How we USE materials

Metal

Rita Storey

A+

Smart Apple Media

This book has been published in cooperation with Franklin Watts.

Series designed and created for Franklin Watts by Painted Fish Ltd., Art director: Jonathan Hair, Designer: Rita Storey, Editor: Fiona Corbridge

Picture credits
Corbis/Duomo p. 23 (bottom), Corbis/Ted Spiegel p. 8, Corbis/Michael S. Yamashita p. 27 (top), Corbis/Bo Zanders p. 9 (bottom); istockphoto.com p. 3, p. 6, p. 7 (top), p. 7 (bottom), p. 9 (top), p. 10, p. 11, p. 12, p. 13, p. 14, p. 15 (middle and bottom), p. 17 (middle), p. 18, p. 19, p. 20, p. 21, p. 22, p. 25 (top), p. 26, p. 27 (bottom); Tudor Photography p. 5, p. 7 (middle), p. 15 (top), p. 16, p. 17 (top and bottom), p. 23 (top), p. 24, p. 25 (bottom).

Cover images: Tudor Photography, Banbury

Published in the United States by Smart Apple Media
2140 Howard Drive West, North Mankato, Minnesota 56003

Library of Congress Cataloging-in-Publication Data

Storey, Rita
Metal / by Rita Storey.
p. cm. – (How we use materials)
Includes index.
ISBN-13: 978-1-59920-003-3
1. Metals—Juvenile literature. 2. Building materials—Juvenile literature. I. Title.

TA459.S75 2007
620.1'6—dc22   2006029884

9 8 7 6 5 4 3 2 1

Contents

Words in **bold** are in the glossary.

What is metal?

Metal is a **natural material**. There are many different types of metal. Most metal is hard.

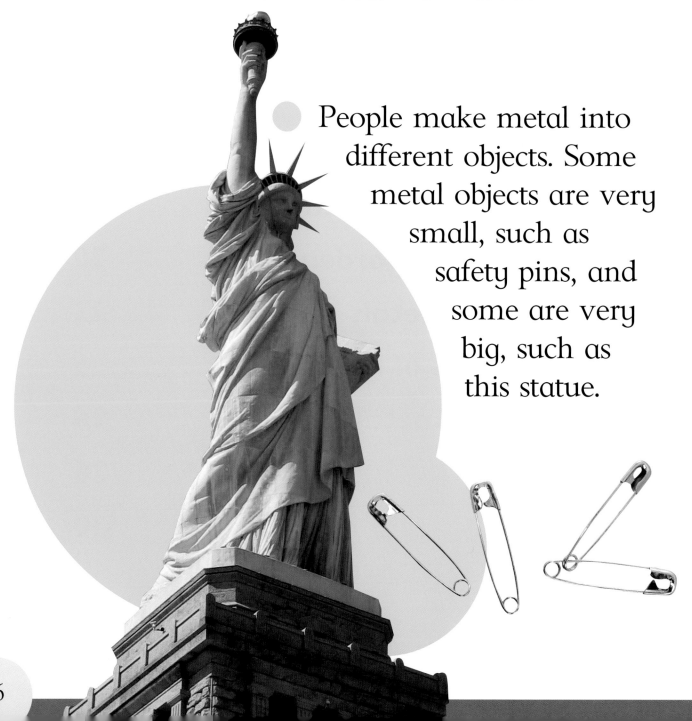

People make metal into different objects. Some metal objects are very small, such as safety pins, and some are very big, such as this statue.

Things made from metal can be very heavy, such as this truck. They can also be very light, such as this soda pop can.

Metal keywords

Hard
Heavy
Light
Strong

Some metal is soft and we can bend it. Some metal is very strong. Parts of this airplane **engine** are made of very strong metal.

Where does metal come from?

Metal is found inside rocks or in the ground. Rocks that have metal in them are called **ores**.

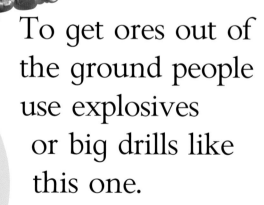

The place where people get ore out of the ground is called a mine.

To get ores out of the ground people use explosives or big drills like this one.

Iron is a metal that comes from iron ore. To get it, iron ore is heated in a very hot oven called a furnace. The metal melts and is collected.

We can find pieces of some metals, such as **gold**, in the earth or in rivers. A lump of gold is called a nugget. This man is trying to find gold nuggets in a river.

nugget

Metal keywords

Ore
Mine
Iron
Gold
Nugget

Building with metal

Metal is strong and can be made into many kinds of shapes. This makes it a good building material.

- Iron is heated until it becomes a **liquid**. Then it is poured into a **mold**. The iron hardens when it cools and takes the shape of the mold.

Metals can be mixed together to make a new metal called an **alloy**. Alloys are very strong.

Iron is mixed with other metals to make an alloy called **steel**. Steel is stronger than iron. It can be shaped in molds to make the **frames** of buildings.

Metal keywords

Alloy
Steel
Mold

Steel can be made into ropes that are strong enough to hold a bridge.

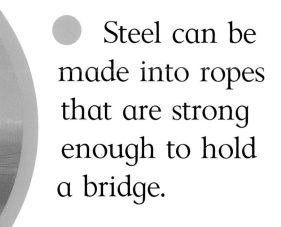

Metal at home

We use metals for different jobs in our homes.

- **Copper** is a reddish-brown metal. It can be bent and shaped easily.

  Copper is used to make pipes that carry water to sinks and baths.

- Nails and screws are made of metal such as steel. They hold things together.

Metal keywords
Copper
Conducts
Brass
Zinc

Metal lets electricity **flow** through it—we say that it **conducts** electricity.

Copper **wires** carry electricity around our homes. Wires carrying electricity are covered in plastic. The plastic stops the electricity from getting out of the wires.

Brass is a mixture of copper and **zinc**. It can be polished to make it shine. These taps are made of brass.

Metal in the kitchen

Look around your kitchen. How many metal objects can you see?

Metal is used to make pans. The metal lets the heat from the stove go through the pan and heat up the food inside. We say that metal conducts heat.

Copper and **aluminum** are good conductors of heat.

Knives, forks, spoons, and cooking tools are made from an alloy called **stainless steel**. It is shiny and easy to wash.

Metal can be made into a tube shape. Tubes are light and strong. They can be bent to make things like this stool.

Metal keywords

Shiny
Stainless steel
Aluminum

Food and drink

Metal is used to make **packaging** for food and drinks.

- Aluminum is a metal. It can be rolled into thin, flexible sheets. These are used to make some soda pop cans.

- Foil is a very thin sheet of aluminum. People buy it on a roll to use in the kitchen. They can wrap food in foil before cooking it. The foil keeps steam in and stops the food from drying out.

Foil containers are good for cooking food. They can be heated up quickly.

Factories use foil for packaging food. It is **waterproof**, **airtight**, and keeps out light. These coffee beans will stay fresh for longer in foil wrapping.

Coffee Beans

Metal keywords
Cans
Foil
Waterproof
Airtight

Food is **sealed** in steel cans. This makes the food last for a long time.

Metal in transportation

Metal is used to make cars, bikes, and airplanes because it is strong.

Steel can be rolled into sheets and bent into different shapes. It is used to make cars.

Air and water make iron and steel **rust**. This means that the metal turns a reddish-brown color and breaks up. Paint helps to stop metal from rusting. On old cars, the paint may crack. Then the metal will rust.

Airplanes have to be strong, but they also need to be light so that they will fly.

Aluminum is light but not very strong. It is mixed with stronger metals to make an alloy that is used for airplanes.

The frame of this bicycle is made of aluminum alloy. It is very light but strong.

Metal in the garden

Metal is useful for making tools and other things we use in the garden.

Iron and steel will rust if they are left outside. If steel is coated with zinc, it does not rust. This steel watering can has a zinc coating.

This ladder is made from aluminum so it is light and easy to carry.

This greenhouse has a frame made of an aluminum alloy, which does not rust. The greenhouse will last for a long time.

Iron can be hammered or bent into shapes like the ones on this gate.

Metal keywords

Coating

Beautiful metals

Metals can be shaped and molded to make beautiful objects.

- Gold, **platinum**, and **silver** are easy to shape and always stay shiny. This makes them good metals for making jewelry such as these bracelets.

Gold has to be mixed with a harder metal before it can be used to make rings like these.

Gold, silver, and **bronze** are used to make **medals**. In many sports, a gold medal like this is the highest prize you can win.

Metal keywords

Platinum
Silver
Bronze

Other uses of metal

Metals are used to make things we use every day.

- Some paint is stored in metal cans. The cans are airtight and stop the paint from drying out.

- Shopping carts and baskets are often made of steel because it does not break.

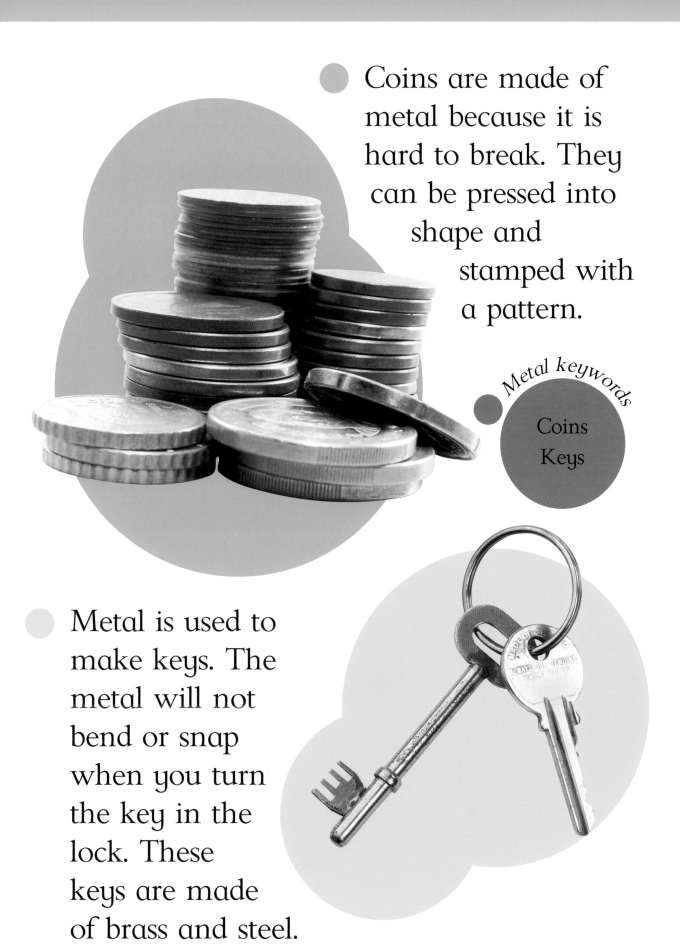

Coins are made of metal because it is hard to break. They can be pressed into shape and stamped with a pattern.

Metal keywords

Coins

Keys

Metal is used to make keys. The metal will not bend or snap when you turn the key in the lock. These keys are made of brass and steel.

Recycling metal

It takes millions of years for metal ores to form in the earth. If we keep taking metal ores to use, they will run out one day.

If we **recycle** metals, we do not need to take so much ore from the ground. It also means we do not need as many mines, which spoil large areas of the countryside. This area used to be a copper mine.

Making new cans uses a lot of **energy**. Instead, we can make new cans from recycled old cans. This uses much less energy.

Some materials pull iron and steel toward them. They are called **magnets**. It is easy to get iron and steel out of a pile of waste metals with a strong magnet. Then the metal can be melted down to make more steel objects.

Metal keywords

Recycling
Magnet

Glossary

Airtight Keeps out the air.

Alloy A metal that is made by mixing two or more metals.

Aluminum A silvery-colored metal. Mixed with other metals to make strong, lightweight objects.

Brass A mixture of zinc and copper.

Bronze A mixture of copper, tin, and zinc.

Conducts Lets something pass from one place to another.

Copper A reddish-brown metal that does not rust.

Energy The power taken from fuel, which is used for light and heat and to move machinery.

Engine The part of a car or airplane that makes it move.

Flow Pass through.

Frames Pieces of metal joined together. Frames are used to help hold up parts of a building.

Gold A shiny, yellow metal.

Iron A metal that is usually mixed with other metals to make steel.

Liquid A material, such as water, that flows.

Magnets Objects that pull iron or steel toward them.

Medals Flat pieces of metal given as a prize.

Mold A shape that liquid metal is poured into to make a different shape.

Natural material Something that comes from the earth, plants, or animals.

Ores Rocks that contain metal.

Packaging Something food and drinks are put in to keep them clean and safe.

Plastic A material made in factories from chemicals.

Platinum A silvery-white metal used for jewelry.

Recycle Use a material again.

Rust A reddish-brown colored coating that makes the metal break up.

Sealed Closed very tightly.

Silver A shiny, grayish-white metal used to make jewelry and medals.

Stainless steel Steel that does not rust or stain.

Steel A very strong alloy of iron.

Waterproof Does not let water pass through.

Wires Long, thin pieces of metal.

Zinc A silvery-blue metal. It is used to cover steel to stop it from rusting.

Index